MAC 'N' CHEESE

MAC 'N' CHEESE

Traditional and inspired recipes for the ultimate comfort food

Laura Washburn photography by Steve Painter

RYLAND PETERS & SMALL

LONDON • NEW YORK

DESIGN, PHOTOGRAPHY AND PROP STYLING
Steve Painter
EDITOR Ellen Parnavelas
HEAD OF PRODUCTION Patricia Harrington
ART DIRECTOR Leslie Harrington
EDITORIAL DIRECTOR Julia Charles

INDEXER Hilary Bird
FOOD STYLIST Lucie McKelvie
FOOD STYLIST'S ASSISTANT Ellie Jarvis

First published in 2013 by
Ryland Peters & Small
20–21 Jockey's Fields
London WC1R 4BW
and
519 Broadway, 5th Floor
New York, NY 10012
www.rylandpeters.com
10 9 8 7 6 5 4

Text © Laura Washburn 2013
Design and photographs
© Ryland Peters & Small 2013

ISBN: 978-1-84975-425-5

A CIP record for this book is available from
the British Library.

US Library of Congress cataloging-in-
Publication Data has been applied for.

Printed in China.

AUTHOR'S ACKNOWLEDGMENTS

Thanks to all those who helped to make this
book so beautiful, especially Steve Painter,
whose photographs are simply inspired. The
idea for this book came from Cindy Richards
at RPS and Cico Books. I could not have
thought of a better idea myself but she got
there first. Thanks also to Julia Charles at RPS
for asking me to carry out the enviable task
of writing it and Ellen Parnavelas for the
thankless task of making it all happen on
time. Heaps of gratitude, however, go to the
Salt-Illingworth family. Over the years, they
have been my cookbook writing guinea pigs.
They have never shied away from whatever
food was on offer, no matter how strange the
combination of dishes. I can always count on
them to arrive, most any time of day, empty
container in hand, to help digest the surplus
which so often results from recipe testing. This
book is dedicated to Kirsten, Steve, Oscar,
Miles and Clarice.

contents

Introduction

What is it that makes mac 'n' cheese so wonderful? For a start, any combination of pasta and melted cheese can hardly be bad, but there is much more to it than that. For many people, mac 'n' cheese is a nostalgic dish of velvety, cheese-smothered noodles that reminds us of home. However, the secret to the perfect mac 'n' cheese is the sum of all its parts, so it is important to consider all the parts separately.

The Pasta

Macaroni is a small, dried pasta shape that is very compact. Some cooks may choose to use other small pasta shapes and this is fine. All the recipes in this book work with either macaroni or other small shapes but my preference is for the original. The hollow space within the tube is really rather small, making it quite a thick and chewy pasta and one that holds the sauce well.

The Sauce

Béchamel sauce is the base of most of the recipes and is not difficult to achieve. Some of the recipes call only for cream, based on nothing more than my discretion. Cream and béchamel can be used interchangeably in all of these recipes, but there are simply some combinations of flavours that go better with cream. The best béchamel sauce for a mac 'n' cheese should not be too thick or the resulting dish will be heavy. Ideally, it should be about as thick as double/heavy cream.

The Cheese

Mac 'n' cheese is all about the cheese. This is where the true flavour comes from, therefore the choice of cheese is crucial. Taste and meltability are the important factors to consider here and will affect the end result. Cheddar and Monterey Jack are reliable, readily available in most places and strong tasting yet still neutral enough to serve as a backdrop for other flavours, so these are good choices. They also melt well. Never be tempted to use ready-grated cheese. The taste is bland, the texture tends to be drier and, often, potato starch or other ingredients are added to prevent sticking and this has an unpleasant effect on the finished dish, making it thick and stodgy.

Cooking Tips

When using macaroni, it is best to slightly overcook the pasta. That way the dish stays moist, as *al dente* pasta tends to soak up some of the sauce, resulting in a drier finished dish. Other pasta shapes are not as thick as macaroni and tend to go limp if overcooked, so cook these shapes as normal, if using. Cook the pasta in lots of well-salted water. Properly seasoned pasta ensures the finished dish will taste great. Be sure, however, to rinse well after cooking to remove excess salt. Excess water thins the texture and dilutes the taste of the finished dish, so drain the pasta thoroughly using a colander that is large enough to hold it all comfortably. If making the dish in advance, drizzle a small amount of vegetable oil over the hot pasta and mix well to prevent sticking before use. Think wide and shallow when choosing a baking dish for you mac 'n' cheese. This will make the surface area as large as possible to allow for more crispy breadcrumb topping and it ensures the dish warms evenly under the grill/broiler.

Classic Macaroni & Cheese

This simple recipe makes a creamy macaroni and cheese that can be used as a base for further experimentation. Combining two mild cheeses, such as Cheddar and Monterey Jack, gives this dish a delicious depth of flavour.

a handful of coarse sea salt

500 g/1 lb. macaroni

50 g/1 cup fresh breadcrumbs

fine sea salt and freshly ground black pepper

FOR THE BÉCHAMEL SAUCE

50 g/3½ tablespoons unsalted butter

60 g/6 tablespoons plain/all-purpose flour

625 ml/2½ cups milk

1 teaspoon fine sea salt

150 g/1¼ cups grated Monterey Jack or other mild, semi-hard cheese

150 g/1¼ cups grated medium Cheddar

SERVES 6–8

Bring a large saucepan of water to the boil. Add the coarse sea salt, then let the water return to a rolling boil. Add the macaroni, stir well and cook according to the package instructions until very tender. Stir periodically to prevent the macaroni from sticking together. When cooked, drain, rinse well under running water and let drip dry in a colander.

Preheat the grill/broiler to medium.

To make the béchamel sauce, melt the butter in a saucepan. Stir in the flour and cook, stirring constantly, for 1 minute. Pour in the milk in a steady stream, whisking constantly, and continue to whisk for 3–5 minutes until the sauce begins to thicken. Season with fine sea salt. Remove from the heat and add the cheeses, mixing well with a spoon to incorporate. Taste and adjust the seasoning.

Put the cooked macaroni in a large mixing bowl. Pour over the hot béchamel sauce and mix well. Taste and adjust the seasoning.

Transfer the macaroni mixture to a baking dish and spread evenly. Top with a good grinding of black pepper and sprinkle the breadcrumbs evenly over the top. Grill/broil for 5–10 minutes until until the top is crunchy and golden brown. Serve immediately.

VEGETABLES

Provençal Tomatoes & Goat Cheese

A taste trio that sings of Mediterranean sunshine, this mac 'n' cheese mélange of thinly sliced goat cheese, thyme-scented cherry tomatoes and fresh basil will transport you straight to the Côte d'Azur. Serve with a crisp green salad dressed with vinaigrette and a chilled bottle of rosé from Provence.

a handful of coarse sea salt

500 g/1 lb. macaroni

500 g/1 lb. cherry tomatoes, halved

a small head of garlic, cloves separated but skins left on

a few sprigs of fresh thyme, chopped

2–3 tablespoons extra virgin olive oil

600 ml/2½ cups double/heavy cream

leaves from a small bunch of fresh basil, thinly sliced

100 g/1¼ cups grated hard goat cheese

2 x 60 g/2 oz. Crottins de Chavignol or other mild goat cheese, ends trimmed and sliced

50 g/1 cup fresh breadcrumbs

fine sea salt and freshly ground black pepper

SERVES 6–8

Cook the macaroni according to the instructions on page 8.

Preheat the oven to 190°C (375°F) Gas 5.

Arrange the halved tomatoes and garlic in a single layer on a baking sheet; some skin side up and some not. Sprinkle over the thyme and oil and toss to coat lightly. Roast in the oven for 15–20 minutes until just charred. Remove the tomatoes and garlic from the oven, slip the garlic cloves out of their skins and chop finely. Set aside. Transfer the tomatoes to a very large bowl and season lightly with salt. Set aside.

Preheat the grill/broiler to medium–hot.

Put the cream in a large saucepan and bring just to the boil, stirring occasionally. Add the basil, chopped garlic and a good pinch of salt, then reduce the heat. Add the grated goat cheese and stir well to melt.

Put the cooked macaroni in the bowl with the tomatoes. Pour over the hot cream sauce and mix well. Taste and adjust the seasoning. Transfer the macaroni mixture to a baking dish and spread evenly. Top with a good grinding of black pepper and arrange the Crottin de Chavignol slices on top of the macaroni. Sprinkle with the breadcrumbs and grill/broil for 5–10 minutes until the top is crunchy and golden brown. Serve immediately.

Roasted Asparagus & Pecorino

Asparagus has such a dominant flavour that it can be difficult to find a suitable partner. However, the equally pervasive Pecorino stands up to the task beautifully. Make this in the spring when fresh asparagus is at its seasonal best.

a handful of coarse sea salt

500 g/1 lb. macaroni

800 g/1 lb. 12 oz. asparagus, trimmed

2–3 tablespoons vegetable oil

zest of 1 lemon, finely grated

1 quantity béchamel sauce (page 8), replacing the Monterey Jack and Cheddar with 200 g/ 2½ cups grated Pecorino

50 g/1 cup fresh breadcrumbs

fine sea salt and freshly ground black pepper

SERVES 6–8

Cook the macaroni according to the instructions on page 8.

Preheat the oven to 200°C (400°F) Gas 6.

Arrange the asparagus in a single layer on a baking sheet, sprinkle over the oil and toss to coat lightly. Roast in the oven for 10–15 minutes until just charred. Remove the asparagus from the oven, cut it in half and put it in a very large bowl. Add the lemon zest, season lightly with salt and set aside.

Preheat the grill/broiler to medium.

Prepare the béchamel sauce according to the instructions on page 8. Remove from the heat and add the cheese, mixing well with a spoon to incorporate. Taste and adjust the seasoning.

Put the cooked macaroni in the bowl with the asparagus. Pour over the hot béchamel sauce and mix well. Taste and adjust the seasoning. Transfer the macaroni mixture to a baking dish and spread evenly. Top with a good grinding of black pepper and sprinkle the breadcrumbs evenly over the top. Grill/broil for 5–10 minutes until the top is crunchy and golden brown. Serve immediately.

Butternut Squash & Sage

Earthy sage and sweet butternut squash are a match made in heaven — even better topped with lashings of cream and melted cheese. This comforting dish is perfect served as a main meal or as an accompaniment to roasted meats.

a handful of coarse sea salt

500 g/1lb. macaroni

1 large butternut squash (1 kg/2 lbs.), skinned, deseeded and cubed

3 tablespoons vegetable oil

30 g/2 tablespoons butter

2 shallots, finely chopped

650 ml/2¾ cups double/heavy cream

leaves from a few sprigs of fresh sage, finely chopped

100 g/1¼ cups grated Padano or Parmesan

100 g/¾ cup grated Cheddar cheese

50 g/1 cup fresh breadcrumbs

fine sea salt and freshly ground black pepper

SERVES 6–8

Cook the macaroni according to the instructions on page 8.

Preheat the oven to 200°C (400°F) Gas 6.

Arrange the squash in a single layer on a baking sheet. Sprinkle over 2 tablespoons of the oil and toss to coat lightly. Roast in the oven for 20–25 minutes until just charred. Remove the squash from the oven and put it in a very large bowl. Season lightly with salt and set aside.

Heat the butter and the remaining oil in a large saucepan. Add the shallots and cook over high heat for 2–3 minutes, or until golden, stirring occasionally. Add the cream, sage and a good pinch of salt and bring to the boil, then reduce the heat. Add the cheeses and stir well to melt.

Preheat the grill/broiler to medium–hot.

Put the cooked macaroni in the bowl with the squash. Pour over the hot cream sauce and mix well. Taste and adjust the seasoning. Transfer the macaroni mixture to a baking dish and spread evenly. Top with a good grinding of black pepper and sprinkle the breadcrumbs evenly over the top. Grill/broil for 5–10 minutes until the top is crunchy and golden brown. Serve immediately.

Caramelized Onions & Smoked Cheese

There are many different types of smoked cheeses, some of which have actually been smoked and those that simply have added smoke flavouring. This no-fuss recipe works well with either, so use whatever is readily available.

a handful of coarse sea salt

500 g/1 lb. macaroni

3 tablespoons vegetable oil

750 g/1½ lbs. onions, red and white, halved and thinly sliced

1 heaped teaspoon light brown sugar

3 tablespoons balsamic vinegar

1 quantity béchamel sauce (page 8), replacing the Monterey Jack with 200 g/1⅔ cups grated smoked cheese and reducing the quantity of grated Cheddar to 100 g/¾ cup

50 g/1 cup fresh breadcrumbs

fine sea salt and freshly ground black pepper

SERVES 6–8

Cook the macaroni according to the instructions on page 8.

Heat the oil in a large frying pan/skillet. Add the onions and cook over high heat for 15–20 minutes until brown and caramelized, stirring occasionally. Add the sugar and vinegar and cook, stirring, until the mixture is almost completely dry; reduce the heat to prevent burning, if necessary. Season with salt and pepper and set aside until needed.

Preheat the grill/broiler to medium.

Prepare the béchamel sauce according to the instructions on page 8. Remove from the heat and add the cheeses, mixing well with a spoon to incorporate. Taste and adjust the seasoning.

Put the cooked macaroni in a large mixing bowl. Add the onions, pour over the hot béchamel sauce and mix well. Taste and adjust the seasoning. Transfer the macaroni mixture to a baking dish and spread evenly. Top with a good grinding of black pepper and sprinkle the breadcrumbs evenly over the top. Grill/broil for 5–10 minutes until the top is crunchy and golden brown. Serve immediately.

Spicy Corn

The best part of this is the way the crunchy sweetness of the fresh corn kernels is complemented by the smoky toasted cumin. Don't be tempted to use frozen or canned corn in this recipe, as it simply will not taste the same.

a handful of coarse sea salt

500 g/1 lb. macaroni

4 corn cobs

1½ teaspoons cumin seeds

1 quantity béchamel sauce (page 8), increasing the quantities of Monterey Jack and Cheddar to 200 g/1⅔ cups each

1 red chilli/chile, finely diced and deseeded, if liked

1 green chilli/chile, finely diced and deseeded,

a few sprigs of fresh coriander/cilantro, finely chopped

50 g/1 cup fresh breadcrumbs

fine sea salt and freshly ground black pepper

SERVES 6-8

Cook the macaroni according to the instructions on page 8.

Bring a large saucepan of water to the boil. Add the corn cobs and cook for 3 minutes. Drain and let cool slightly, then scrape off the kernels with a sharp knife and set aside.

Heat a small frying pan/skillet until hot but not smoking. Add the cumin seeds and cook until aromatic and beginning to brown. Transfer to a dish to cool, then grind to a powder with a mortar and pestle and set aside.

Preheat the grill/broiler to medium.

Prepare the béchamel sauce according to the instructions on page 8. Remove from the heat and add the cheeses, chillies/chiles and cumin, mixing well with a spoon to incorporate. Taste and adjust the seasoning.

Put the cooked macaroni in a large mixing bowl. Add the corn and coriander/cilantro, pour over the hot béchamel sauce and mix well. Taste and adjust the seasoning. Transfer the macaroni mixture to a baking dish and spread evenly. Top with a good grinding of black pepper and sprinkle the breadcrumbs evenly over the top. Grill/broil for 5–10 minutes until the top is crunchy and golden brown. Serve immediately.

Jalapeño, Tomato & Monterey Jack

Cheese and chilli/chile are time-honoured companions and this recipe carries on the tradition. This delicious dish is quick to prepare and is perfect for a late-night supper or weekend brunch.

a handful of coarse sea salt

500 g/1 lb. macaroni

1 quantity béchamel sauce (page 8), adjusting the quantities of the cheeses to 200 g/1⅔ cups grated Monterey Jack and 100 g/¾ cup grated Cheddar

80 g/1 x 3-oz. can jalapeños, chopped

300 g/10 oz. cherry tomatoes, chopped

a few sprigs of fresh coriander/cilantro, finely chopped

50 g/1 cup fresh breadcrumbs

fine sea salt and freshly ground black pepper

SERVES 6-8

Cook the macaroni according to the instructions on page 8.

Preheat the grill/broiler to medium–hot.

Prepare the béchamel sauce according to the instructions on page 8. Remove from the heat and add the cheeses, mixing well with a spoon to incorporate. Taste and adjust the seasoning.

Put the cooked macaroni in a large mixing bowl. Add the jalapeños, tomatoes and coriander/cilantro. Pour over the hot béchamel sauce and mix well. Taste and adjust the seasoning. Transfer the macaroni mixture to a baking dish and spread evenly. Top with a good grinding of black pepper and sprinkle the breadcrumbs evenly over the top. Grill/broil for 5–10 minutes until the top is crunchy and golden brown. Serve immediately.

Chard & Gruyère

The nutty taste of Gruyère goes beautifully with leafy greens such as chard, but if this is unavailable, fresh spinach is a very good replacement. This dish can be served as a main meal or as an accompaniment.

a handful of coarse sea salt

500 g/1 lb. macaroni

400 g/14 oz. chard, trimmed

3–4 tablespoons unsalted butter or vegetable oil

1 quantity béchamel sauce (page 8), replacing the Monterey Jack and Cheddar with 350 g/ 3 cups finely grated Gruyère

50 g/1 cup fresh breadcrumbs

fine sea salt and freshly ground black pepper

SERVES 6–8

Cook the macaroni according to the instructions on page 8.

Preheat the grill/broiler to medium–hot.

Put the chard in a large heatproof bowl and add boiling water to cover. Let stand for 3–5 minutes to blanch, then drain well. Squeeze the chard to remove excess moisture and chop coarsely.

Heat the butter or oil in a frying pan/skillet. Add the chard and cook over medium heat until wilted, stirring often. Season with salt and pepper and set aside.

Prepare the béchamel sauce according to the instructions on page 8. Remove from the heat and add the Gruyère, mixing well with a spoon to incorporate. Taste and adjust the seasoning.

Put the cooked macaroni in a large mixing bowl. Stir in the chard, pour over the hot béchamel sauce and mix well. Taste and adjust the seasoning. Transfer the macaroni mixture to a baking dish and spread evenly. Top with a good grinding of black pepper and sprinkle the breadcrumbs evenly over the top. Grill/broil for 5–10 minutes until the top is crunchy and golden brown. Serve immediately.

NOTE: If using Swiss chard, separate the white and green parts and blanch the whites in a saucepan of boiling water, as these take slightly longer to soften.

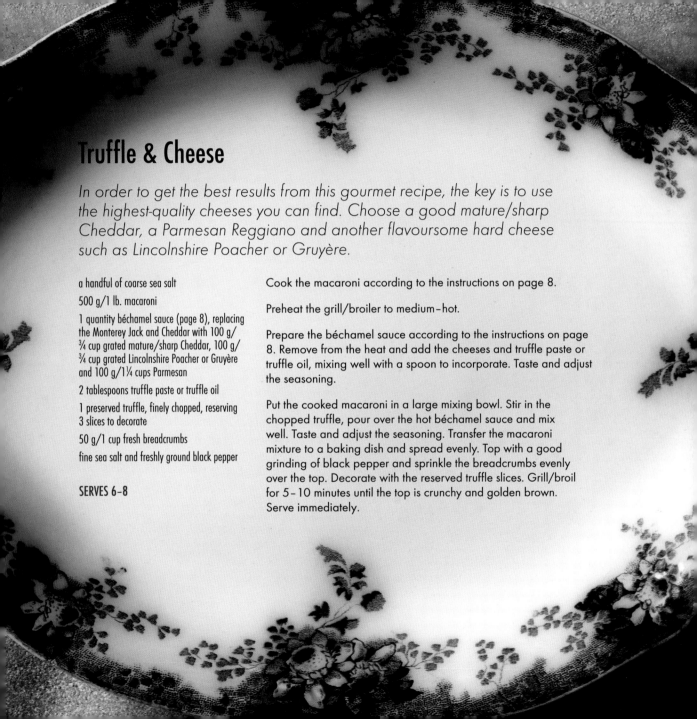

Truffle & Cheese

In order to get the best results from this gourmet recipe, the key is to use the highest-quality cheeses you can find. Choose a good mature/sharp Cheddar, a Parmesan Reggiano and another flavoursome hard cheese such as Lincolnshire Poacher or Gruyère.

a handful of coarse sea salt

500 g/1 lb. macaroni

1 quantity béchamel sauce (page 8), replacing the Monterey Jack and Cheddar with 100 g/¾ cup grated mature/sharp Cheddar, 100 g/¾ cup grated Lincolnshire Poacher or Gruyère and 100 g/1¼ cups Parmesan

2 tablespoons truffle paste or truffle oil

1 preserved truffle, finely chopped, reserving 3 slices to decorate

50 g/1 cup fresh breadcrumbs

fine sea salt and freshly ground black pepper

SERVES 6–8

Cook the macaroni according to the instructions on page 8.

Preheat the grill/broiler to medium–hot.

Prepare the béchamel sauce according to the instructions on page 8. Remove from the heat and add the cheeses and truffle paste or truffle oil, mixing well with a spoon to incorporate. Taste and adjust the seasoning.

Put the cooked macaroni in a large mixing bowl. Stir in the chopped truffle, pour over the hot béchamel sauce and mix well. Taste and adjust the seasoning. Transfer the macaroni mixture to a baking dish and spread evenly. Top with a good grinding of black pepper and sprinkle the breadcrumbs evenly over the top. Decorate with the reserved truffle slices. Grill/broil for 5–10 minutes until the top is crunchy and golden brown. Serve immediately.

Aubergine Parmigiana

This mac 'n' cheese interpretation of a classic Italian dish is always a crowd pleaser. Here, the aubergine/eggplant is roasted, giving it a lovely, crisp texture.

a handful of coarse sea salt

500 g/1 lb. macaroni

4–5 tablespoons vegetable oil

1 large onion, finely chopped

1 teaspoon dried thyme

1 teaspoon dried oregano

1 teaspoon dried rosemary

3 garlic cloves, finely chopped

1 x 400-g/14-oz. can chopped tomatoes

1 medium aubergine/eggplant, sliced

1 quantity béchamel sauce (page 8) replacing the Monterey Jack and Cheddar with 100 g/¾ cup grated Fontina and 100 g/1¼ cups grated Parmesan

125 g/1 cup shredded mozzarella

leaves from 2–3 sprigs fresh basil, coarsely torn

50 g/1 cup fresh breadcrumbs

fine sea salt and freshly ground black pepper

SERVES 6–8

Cook the macaroni according to the instructions on page 8.

Preheat the oven to 200°C (400°F) Gas 6.

Heat 2 tablespoons of the oil in a large sauté pan with a lid. Add the onion and cook over medium heat for 5 minutes until just golden. Stir in the herbs and garlic and cook gently for 1 minute, taking care not to let the garlic burn. Add the tomatoes and 1 teaspoon of fine sea salt and simmer very gently for 20–30 minutes until very thick.

Arrange the aubergine/eggplant slices in a single layer on a baking sheet and sprinkle over the remaining oil. Roast for 15–20 minutes until tender and just charred. Remove, season lightly with salt and add to the tomatoes. Simmer gently while you prepare the béchamel sauce.

Preheat the grill/broiler to medium.

Prepare the béchamel sauce according to the instructions on page 8. Remove from the heat and add the Fontina and Parmesan, mixing well with a spoon to incorporate. Taste and adjust the seasoning.

Put the cooked macaroni in a large mixing bowl. Stir in the aubergine/eggplant mixture, pour over the hot béchamel sauce and mix well. Taste and adjust the seasoning. Transfer the macaroni mixture to a baking dish and spread evenly. Top with the mozzarella, the basil leaves and a good grinding of black pepper and sprinkle the breadcrumbs evenly over the top. Grill/broil for 5–10 minutes until the top is crunchy and golden brown. Serve immediately.

Mushroom, Tarragon & Taleggio

It is the tarragon in this recipe that transforms it from an ordinary mushroom and cheese dish into something truly sublime. Be sure to use the fresh herb, as dried is simply not the same.

a handful of coarse sea salt

500 g/1 lb. macaroni

300 g/10 oz. Portobello mushrooms, stems trimmed level with cap

2–3 tablespoons vegetable oil

leaves from a few sprigs of fresh parsley, finely chopped

leaves from a few sprigs of fresh tarragon, finely chopped

600 ml/2½ cups double/heavy cream

100 g/¾ cup grated Cheddar

50 g/⅔ cup grated Parmesan

250 g/8 oz. Taleggio, thinly sliced

fine sea salt and freshly ground black pepper

SERVES 6–8

Cook the macaroni according to the instructions on page 8.

Preheat the oven to 200°C (400°F) Gas 6.

Arrange the mushrooms in a single layer on a baking sheet, stems up, and brush with the oil. Season lightly with salt, sprinkle over the herbs and roast for 15–20 minutes until tender. Remove and let cool slightly. Slice the mushrooms and set aside.

Preheat the grill/broiler to medium.

Put the cream in a large saucepan and bring just to the boil, stirring occasionally, then reduce the heat. Add the Cheddar and Parmesan and half the Taleggio, and stir well to melt. Taste and adjust the seasoning.

Put the cooked macaroni in a large mixing bowl. Stir in half the sliced mushrooms, pour over the hot cream sauce and mix well. Taste and adjust the seasoning. Transfer the macaroni mixture to a baking dish and spread evenly. Top with the remaining mushrooms and Taleggio slices and a good grinding of black pepper. Grill/broil for 5–10 minutes until the top is golden and serve immediately.

FISH

Salmon, Basil & Parmesan

Like a mac 'n' cheese fish pie, this hearty and nutritious recipe makes a perfect weeknight meal for anyone with a healthy appetite. Serve with plenty of fresh green vegetables such as barely-blanched peas or steamed broccoli florets.

a handful of coarse sea salt

500 g/1 lb. macaroni

500 g/1 lb. boneless, skinless salmon fillets

600 ml/2½ cups double/heavy cream

leaves from a small bunch of fresh basil, chopped, reserving a few whole leaves to serve

200 g/1⅔ cups grated medium Cheddar

100 g/1¼ cups grated Parmesan

50 g/1 cup fresh breadcrumbs

fine sea salt and freshly ground black pepper

SERVES 6–8

Cook the macaroni according to the instructions on page 8.

Preheat the oven to 200°C (400°F) Gas 6.

Arrange the salmon fillets in a single layer on a baking sheet and bake until cooked through and the flesh flakes easily. Remove and let cool slightly.

Preheat the grill/broiler to medium–hot.

Put the cream and chopped basil in a saucepan and bring just to the boil, stirring occasionally. Remove from the heat, add the cheeses and stir well to melt.

Flake the salmon and put it in a large bowl. Add the cooked macaroni, pour over the hot cream sauce and mix well. Taste and adjust the seasoning. Transfer the macaroni mixture to a baking dish and spread evenly. Top with a good grinding of black pepper and sprinkle the breadcrumbs evenly over the top. Grill/broil for 5–10 minutes until the top is crunchy and golden brown. Scatter over the remaining basil leaves and serve immediately.

Crab Gratin

This dish is based on a traditional English recipe for crab gratin and has a unique flavour as a result of combining quintessentially English ingredients such as Worcestershire sauce, sherry and mustard powder. Be sure to use a mixture of brown and white crab meat – the result will be elegant and sophisticated and, dare it be said, fit for royalty.

a handful of coarse sea salt

500 g/1 lb. macaroni

60 g/4 tablespoons unsalted butter

1 large onion, finely chopped

3 tablespoons dry sherry

60 g/½ cup plain/all-purpose flour

375 ml/1½ cups milk

3 teaspoons Worcestershire sauce

2 heaped teaspoons English mustard powder

1–2 teaspoons ground cayenne pepper

250 g/1 cup crème fraîche/sour cream

250 g/2 cups grated mild cheese, such as Cheddar

400 g/14 oz. lump crab meat, a combination of brown and white

freshly squeezed juice of ½ lemon

50 g/1 cup fresh breadcrumbs

fine sea salt and freshly ground black pepper

SERVES 6–8

Cook the macaroni according to the instructions on page 8.

Preheat the grill/broiler to medium-hot.

Melt the butter in a large saucepan. Add the onion and cook over medium heat for 5–10 minutes until soft. Add the sherry and cook until the liquid has evaporated, stirring continuously. Stir in the flour and cook for 1 minute, then add the milk, whisking constantly, until the mixture thickens. Stir in the Worcestershire sauce, mustard powder, cayenne pepper, ½ teaspoon of fine sea salt and crème fraîche/sour cream until well blended, then stir in the cheese, crab and lemon juice.

Put the cooked macaroni in a large mixing bowl. Pour over the hot cheese and crab sauce and mix well. Taste and adjust the seasoning, adding more salt, lemon juice or cayenne pepper as desired. Transfer the macaroni mixture to a baking dish and spread evenly. Top with a good grinding of black pepper and sprinkle the breadcrumbs evenly over the top. Grill/broil for 5–10 minutes until the top is crunchy and golden brown. Serve immediately.

Tuna & Mushroom

This nostalgic dish is retro in spirit, taking inspiration from an old-fashioned American classic: the tuna noodle casserole. So quick and easy, it calls for only the most basic of ingredients, most of which should be on hand in any well-stocked kitchen.

a handful of coarse sea salt

500 g/1 lb. macaroni

2-3 tablespoons vegetable oil

1 small onion, finely chopped

100 g/3½ oz. mushrooms, chopped

1 celery stalk, finely chopped

1 quantity béchamel sauce (page 8), omitting the Monterey Jack

350 g/12 oz. canned tuna in brine, drained and flaked

a small bunch of fresh flat leaf parsley, finely chopped

50 g/1 cup fresh breadcrumbs

2 tablespoons grated Parmesan

fine sea salt and freshly ground black pepper

SERVES 6-8

Cook the macaroni according to the instructions on page 8.

Heat the oil in a large frying pan/skillet. Add the onion, mushrooms and celery and cook over high heat for about 5 minutes until golden, stirring occasionally. Season with salt and pepper and set aside.

Preheat the grill/broiler to medium-hot.

Prepare the béchamel sauce according to the instructions on page 8. Remove from the heat and add the Cheddar, mixing well with a spoon to incorporate. Taste and adjust the seasoning.

Put the cooked macaroni in a large mixing bowl with the tuna, mushroom mixture and parsley. Pour over the hot béchamel sauce and mix well. Taste and adjust the seasoning.

In a small bowl, mix together the breadcrumbs and Parmesan. Set aside.

Transfer the macaroni mixture to a baking dish and spread evenly. Top with a good grinding of black pepper and sprinkle the breadcrumb mixture evenly over the top. Grill/broil for 5-10 minutes until the top is crunchy and golden brown. Serve immediately.

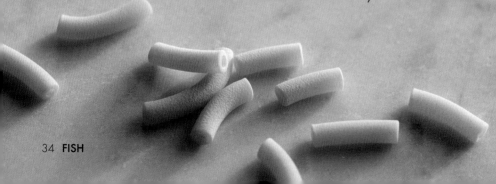

Lobster Thermidor

It is difficult to fathom pairing shellfish with cheese, but this classic dish proves it can be done, with immense success. The key is the combination of mustard, Gruyère and tarragon alongside the sweetness of the lobster. Ask your fishmonger to cook and prepare the lobster meat for you or use frozen lobster tails.

Cook the macaroni according to the instructions on page 8.

Preheat the grill/broiler to medium–hot.

Melt the butter in a large saucepan over medium heat. Add the shallot and cook for 5 minutes until soft. Add the sherry and cook until the liquid has almost evaporated, stirring continuously. Stir in the flour and cook for 1 minute, then add the milk, whisking constantly, until the mixture thickens. Stir in the mustard, cayenne pepper, ½ teaspoon of fine sea salt, tarragon and crème fraîche/sour cream until well blended. Stir in the cheeses and lobster. Taste and adjust the seasoning.

Put the cooked macaroni in a large mixing bowl. Pour over the hot cheese and lobster sauce and mix well. Taste and adjust the seasoning. Transfer the macaroni mixture to a baking dish and spread evenly. Top with a good grinding of black pepper and sprinkle the breadcrumbs evenly over the top. Grill/broil for 5–10 minutes until the top is crunchy and golden brown. Serve immediately.

a handful of coarse sea salt

500 g/1 lb. macaroni

60 g/4 tablespoons unsalted butter

1 large shallot, finely chopped

3 tablespoons dry sherry

60 g/½ cup plain/all-purpose flour

400 ml/1⅔ cups milk

2 heaped teaspoons English mustard powder

1 teaspoon ground cayenne pepper

leaves from 2 sprigs of fresh tarragon, finely chopped

250 g/1 cup crème fraîche/sour cream

200 g/1⅔ cups grated Gruyère

50 g/⅔ cup grated Parmesan

750 g/1¾ lbs. cooked lobster meat

50 g/1 cup fresh breadcrumbs

fine sea salt and freshly ground black pepper

SERVES 6–8

Smoked Haddock & Spinach

Delicate smoked haddock and wilted spinach are a classic combination that needs nothing more than a light creamy sauce spiced with nutmeg to make the flavours sing, resulting in an impressive dish indeed. Lovely for a light dinner or even a weekend brunch.

a handful of coarse sea salt

500 g/1 lb. macaroni

600 g/1¼ lbs. smoked haddock fillets

2 tablespoons vegetable oil

500 g/1 lb. fresh spinach

15 g/1 tablespoon unsalted butter

1 large shallot, finely chopped

600 ml/2½ cups double/heavy cream

a pinch of grated nutmeg

200 g/1⅔ cups grated medium Cheddar

50 g/1 cup fresh breadcrumbs

fine sea salt and freshly ground black pepper

SERVES 6-8

Cook the macaroni according to the instructions on page 8.

Arrange the haddock fillets in a microwaveable dish in a single layer, skin side down, and pour over just enough water to cover. Cover with clingfilm/plastic wrap and microwave on high for 4–5 minutes, or until the flesh flakes easily. Flake the fish, discard the skin and cooking liquid and remove any bones. Set aside.

Heat 1 tablespoon of the oil in a deep frying pan/skillet. Add half the spinach and cook over high heat, stirring often, until wilted. Season lightly with salt and pepper, then transfer to a chopping board and spread out to cool. Repeat for the remaining spinach, then chop all the spinach coarsely and set aside in a large mixing bowl.

Preheat the grill/broiler to medium–hot.

In the same large skillet/frying pan, melt the butter and heat the remaining oil. Add the shallot and cook over high heat for 2–3 minutes until just golden, stirring occasionally. Add the cream, nutmeg and a good pinch of salt and bring just to the boil, then reduce the heat.

Add the haddock and cheese to the spinach in the bowl and pour over the hot cream mixture. Stir well to melt the cheese, then add the macaroni and mix well. Taste and adjust the seasoning.

Transfer the macaroni mixture to a baking dish and spread evenly. Top with a good grinding of black pepper and sprinkle the breadcrumbs evenly over the top. Grill/broil for 5–10 minutes until the top is crunchy and golden brown. Serve immediately

Shrimp & Feta

Inspired by a traditional Greek dish, this is simple yet elegant and as good for a quick midweek supper as it is for impressive entertaining.

a handful of coarse sea salt

500 g/1 lb. macaroni

2–3 tablespoons vegetable oil

1 large onion, finely diced

350 g/12 oz. raw prawns/shrimp

1 teaspoon dried thyme

1 teaspoon dried oregano

2 garlic cloves, crushed

1 x 400-g/14-oz. can chopped tomatoes

1 quantity béchamel sauce (page 8), replacing the Monterey Jack with 100 g/1¼ cups grated Graviera or Kasseri and increasing the quantity of Cheddar to 200 g/1⅔ cups

100 g/⅔ cup crumbled feta

50 g/1 cup fresh breadcrumbs

fine sea salt and freshly ground black pepper

SERVES 6–8

Cook the macaroni according to the instructions on page 8.

Heat the oil in a large sauté pan with a lid. Add the onion and cook over medium heat for 5 minutes until just golden. Stir in the prawns/shrimp, thyme, oregano and ½ teaspoon of fine sea salt and cook until the prawns/shrimp just turn pink. Add the garlic and cook gently for 1 minute, taking care not to let it burn. Add the tomatoes and a grinding of black pepper and simmer very gently for about 15–30 minutes until the mixture has reduced to a jam-like consistency.

Preheat the grill/broiler to medium.

Prepare the béchamel sauce according to the instructions on page 8. Remove from the heat and add the cheeses, mixing well with a spoon to incorporate. Taste and adjust the seasoning.

Put the cooked macaroni in a large mixing bowl. Pour over the hot béchamel sauce and mix well. Taste the prawn/shrimp mixture and adjust the seasoning as necessary. Add to the macaroni and mix well. Transfer the macaroni mixture to a baking dish and spread evenly. Sprinkle over the feta and scatter the breadcrumbs evenly over the top. Grill/broil for 5–10 minutes until the top is crunchy and golden brown. Serve immediately.

MEAT

Spicy Beef

Brimming with pasta, beef and béchamel sauce, this hearty dish is like lasagne with a spicy southwestern twist. Feel free to turn up the heat by adding a chopped fresh green chilli/chile to the meat when browning.

a handful of coarse sea salt

500 g/1 lb. macaroni

2 tablespoons vegetable oil

1 large onion, finely diced

1 red (bell) pepper, finely diced

½ teaspoon dried chilli/hot pepper flakes

¼ teaspoon ground cayenne pepper

2 teaspoons ground cumin

1½ teaspoons dried oregano

400 g/14 oz. minced/ground beef

1 x 400-g/14-oz. can chopped tomatoes

1 quantity béchamel sauce (see page 8)

50 g/1 cup fresh breadcrumbs

fine sea salt and freshly ground black pepper

SERVES 6–8

Cook the macaroni according to the instructions on page 8.

Heat the oil in a large frying pan/skillet. Add the onion and cook over high heat for 3–5 minutes, stirring occasionally. Add the red pepper, spices and oregano and cook for 3–5 minutes, or until soft and golden. Add the beef and 1 teaspoon of the sea salt. Stir to break up the meat and cook until well browned, stirring often. Stir in the tomatoes and simmer gently for about 15 minutes.

Preheat the grill/broiler to medium–hot.

Prepare the béchamel sauce according to the instructions on page 8. Taste and adjust the seasoning.

Put the cooked macaroni in a large mixing bowl. Pour over the hot béchamel sauce and mix well.

Taste the beef mixture and adjust the seasoning, adding more dried chilli/hot pepper flakes if desired. Add to the macaroni mixture and mix well. Taste and adjust the seasoning.

Transfer the macaroni mixture to a baking dish and spread evenly. Top with a good grinding of black pepper and sprinkle the breadcrumbs evenly over the top. Grill/broil for 5–10 minutes until browned and serve immediately.

Greek Lamb

The combination of spices here is based on the traditional recipe for Moussaka, a Greek dish made with lamb and aubergines/eggplant. Serve with a Greek salad made with cucumber, tomatoes, feta and olives.

a handful of coarse sea salt

500 g/1 lb. macaroni

2 tablespoons vegetable oil

1 large onion, finely diced

1 red (bell) pepper, sliced

1 teaspoon ground cinnamon

¼ teaspoon ground cayenne pepper

2 teaspoons ground cumin

1½ teaspoons dried oregano

400 g/14 oz. minced/ground lamb

1 x 400-g/14-oz. can chopped tomatoes

1 quantity béchamel sauce (see page 8), replacing the Monterey Jack with 100 g/1¼ cups grated Graviera or Kasseri and increasing the quantity of Cheddar to 200 g/1⅔ cups

100 g/⅔ cup crumbled feta

50 g/1 cup fresh breadcrumbs

fine sea salt and freshly ground black pepper

SERVES 6–8

Cook the macaroni according to the instructions on page 8.

Heat the oil in a large skillet/frying pan. Add the onion and cook over high heat for about 5 minutes until golden, stirring occasionally. Add the red pepper, spices and oregano and cook for 3–5 minutes, until soft. Add the lamb and 1 teaspoon of fine sea salt. Stir to break up the meat and cook until well browned, stirring often. Stir in the tomatoes and simmer gently for 15–30 minutes.

Preheat the grill/broiler to medium.

Prepare the béchamel sauce according to the instructions on page 8. Remove from the heat and add the cheeses, mixing well with a spoon to incorporate. Taste and adjust the seasoning.

Put the cooked macaroni in a large mixing bowl. Pour over the hot béchamel sauce and mix well.

Taste the lamb mixture and adjust the seasoning, adding more spices if desired. Add to the macaroni mixture and mix well. Taste and adjust the seasoning.

Transfer the macaroni mixture to a baking dish and spread evenly. Sprinkle over the feta, then top with the breadcrumbs. Grill/broil for 5–10 minutes until browned. Serve immediately.

Frankfurters, Onions & Mustard

a handful of coarse sea salt

500 g/1 lb. macaroni

2 tablespoons vegetable oil

1 large onion, coarsely chopped

350–400 g/12–14 oz. frankfurters/hot dogs (about 8–10), sliced into bite-size pieces

1 quantity béchamel sauce (page 8), replacing the Monterey Jack and Cheddar with 300 g/2½ cups grated Red Leicester

2 heaped tablespoons wholegrain mustard

50 g/1 cup fresh breadcrumbs

fine sea salt and freshly ground black pepper

wholegrain mustard, to serve

SERVES 6–8

For best results, be sure to use both good-quality frankfurters/hot dogs and flavoursome cheese. Red Leicester works well here, both for its tangy taste and orange hue. If unavailable, a strong/sharp Cheddar used in combination with a milder orange-coloured hard cheese will also work. Serve with extra wholegrain mustard on the side.

Cook the macaroni according to the instructions on page 8.

Heat the oil in a large frying pan/skillet. Add the onion and cook over high heat for 5–8 minutes until brown and caramelized, stirring occasionally. Season lightly with salt and pepper. Add the frankfurter/hot dog pieces and cook for 2–3 minutes until just browned. Set aside.

Prepare the béchamel sauce according to the instructions on page 0. Remove from the heat and add the cheeses and the mustard, mixing well with a spoon to incorporate. Taste and adjust the seasoning.

Put the cooked macaroni in a large mixing bowl. Pour over the hot béchamel sauce, stir in the frankfurter/hot dog mixture and mix well. Taste and adjust the seasoning. Transfer the macaroni mixture to a baking dish and spread evenly. Top with a good grinding of black pepper and sprinkle the breadcrumbs evenly over the top. Grill/broil for 5–10 minutes until the top is crunchy and golden brown. Serve immediately.

Chorizo, Sweet Pepper & Manchego

A combination of Spanish flavours come together here for a mac 'n' cheese fiesta. Manchego is a salty, intensely flavoured Spanish cheese made from sheep's milk. If this is unavailable, replace with Pecorino or more Cheddar.

a handful of coarse sea salt

500 g/1 lb. macaroni

2 tablespoons vegetable oil

1 large onion, finely chopped

1 red (bell) pepper, sliced

250 g/8 oz. chorizo, sliced

1 garlic clove, crushed

1 teaspoon dried thyme

1 x 400-g/14-oz. can chopped tomatoes

1 quantity béchamel sauce (page 8), replacing the Monterey Jack with 150 g/1¼ cups finely grated Manchego and increasing the quantity of Cheddar to 200 g/1⅔ cups

50 g/1 cup fresh breadcrumbs

fine sea salt and freshly ground black pepper

SERVES 6–8

Cook the macaroni according to the instructions on page 8.

Heat the oil in a large sauté pan with a lid. Add the onion and red pepper and cook over medium heat for about 5 minutes until the onion is just golden. Add the chorizo and cook for 2–3 minutes until browned, stirring occasionally. Stir in the garlic, thyme and ½ teaspoon of fine sea salt and cook gently for 1 minute, taking care not to let the garlic burn. Add the tomatoes, a grinding of black pepper and simmer very gently for 15–30 minutes until the mixture has reduced to a jam-like consistency. Taste and adjust the seasoning, then set aside.

Preheat the grill/broiler to medium.

Prepare the béchamel sauce according to the instructions on page 8. Remove from the heat and add 100 g/¾ cup of the Manchego and the Cheddar, mixing well with a spoon to incorporate. Taste and adjust the seasoning.

Put the cooked macaroni in a large mixing bowl. Pour over the hot béchamel sauce, add the chorizo mixture and mix well. Taste and adjust the seasoning.

In a small bowl, toss together the breadcrumbs, the remaining Manchego and a grinding of black pepper. Set aside.

Transfer the macaroni mixture to a baking dish and spread evenly. Top with a good grinding of black pepper and sprinkle the breadcrumb mixture evenly over the top. Grill/broil for 5–10 minutes until the top is crunchy and golden brown. Serve immediately.

Reblochon, Leek & Bacon

This delicious French-inspired mac 'n' cheese combines the traditional ingredients of the classic Alpine dish Tartiflette. Its hearty and elegant flavours make it perfect for entertaining. Serve with a crisp white wine from the Savoie region of France, in keeping with the origins of the dish.

Cook the macaroni according to the instructions on page 8.

Preheat the oven to 180°C (350°F) Gas 4.

Arrange the leeks in a single layer on a baking sheet. Sprinkle over 2 tablespoons of the oil and toss to coat lightly. Roast in the oven for about 15 minutes until tender and just charred. Remove the leeks from the oven and transfer to a very large bowl. Season lightly with salt and set aside.

Heat the remaining oil in a sauté pan. Add the bacon and cook over medium–high heat for 5–10 minutes until well browned. Drain away the excess fat and add to the leeks in the bowl.

Preheat the grill/broiler to medium–hot.

Combine the cream and crème fraîche/sour cream in a large saucepan and bring just to the boil, stirring occasionally. Remove from the heat, add the grated cheese and diced Reblochon and stir well to melt.

Put the cooked macaroni in the bowl with the leeks. Pour over the hot cream sauce and mix well. Taste and adjust the seasoning. Transfer the macaroni mixture to a baking dish and spread evenly. Arrange the remaining Reblochon slices on top, finish with a good grinding of black pepper and sprinkle the breadcrumbs evenly over the top. Grill/broil for 5–10 minutes until the top is crunchy and golden brown. Serve immediately.

a handful of coarse sea salt

500 g/1 lb. macaroni

3 large leeks (about 500 g/1 lb.), sliced into rounds

3 tablespoons vegetable oil

200 g/7 oz. bacon lardons

300 ml/1¼ cups double/heavy cream

300 g/1¼ cups crème fraîche/sour cream

100 g/¾ cup grated mild Cheddar or Monterey Jack

250 g/8 oz. Reblochon or other rich, soft cow's milk cheese such as Brie, half finely diced and half thinly sliced

50 g/1 cup fresh breadcrumbs

fine sea salt and freshly ground black pepper

SERVES 6-8

Mini Meatballs with Mozzarella

Dotted with tiny bite-size meatballs, this is a very family friendly dish with gentle flavours and not too spicy. It is very easy to prepare in advance, making it a great weeknight dinner, and is substantial enough to be a meal in itself. Serve with a simple green salad.

a handful of coarse sea salt

500 g/1 lb. macaroni

1 quantity béchamel sauce (page 8)

150 g/5 oz. fresh mozzarella, drained and torn into bite-size pieces

fine sea salt and freshly ground black pepper

TOMATO SAUCE

2 tablespoons olive oil

1 small onion, finely chopped

1 teaspoon dried rosemary

1 garlic clove, finely chopped

1 x 400-g/14-oz can chopped tomatoes

a pinch of sugar

FOR THE MEATBALLS

500 g/1 lb. minced/ground beef

20 g/⅓ cup fresh breadcrumbs

1 teaspoon dried thyme

2 teaspoons Worcestershire sauce

1 tablespoon tomato ketchup

3 tablespoons milk

SERVES 6–8

Cook the macaroni according to the instructions on page 8.

To make the tomato sauce, heat the oil in a large sauté pan with a lid. Add the onion and cook over medium heat for about 5 minutes until just golden. Stir in the rosemary, garlic and 1 teaspoon of fine sea salt. Cook gently for 1 minute, taking care not to let the garlic burn. Add the tomatoes and sugar and simmer very gently, stirring occasionally, while you prepare the meatballs.

To make the meatballs, put all the ingredients in a large bowl, season with salt and pepper and mix thoroughly with your hands. If the mixture is very dry, add another tablespoon of milk; it should be soft so that the meatballs have a smooth and not crumbly texture. Shape the meat mixture into small balls, about the size of grapes.

Taste the sauce for seasoning and adjust as necessary. Arrange the meatballs in a single layer in the sauce, cover and simmer gently for about 20 minutes until cooked through.

Prepare the béchamel sauce according to the instructions on page 8. Taste and adjust the seasoning.

Preheat the oven to 180°C (350°F) Gas 4.

Put the cooked macaroni in a large mixing bowl. Pour over the hot béchamel sauce and mix well. Transfer the macaroni mixture to a baking dish and sprinkle over the mozzarella pieces. Spoon over the meatballs and tomato sauce in an even layer and mix the meatballs into the macaroni gently with a large wooden or metal spoon. The mixtures do not have to blend completely; some of the meatball mixture should be visible on the top. Bake for 20–30 minutes until golden and bubbling. Serve immediately.

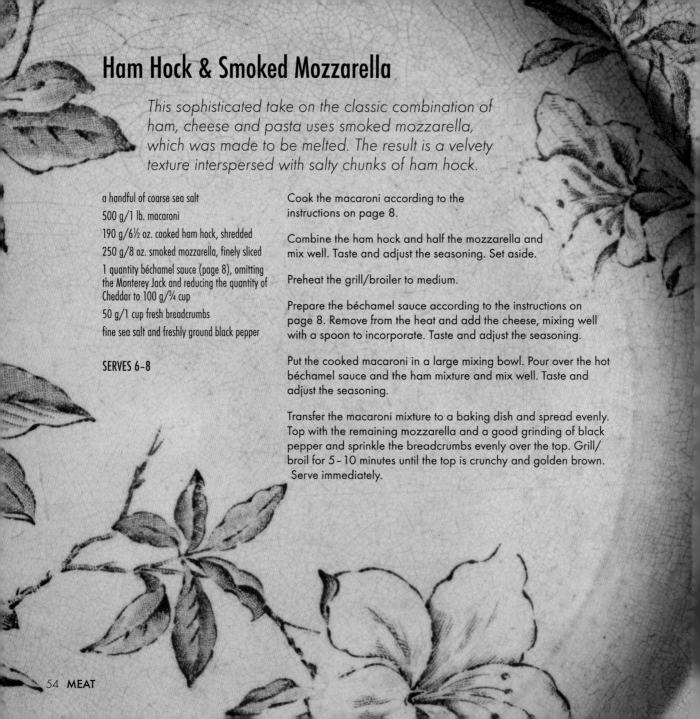

Ham Hock & Smoked Mozzarella

This sophisticated take on the classic combination of ham, cheese and pasta uses smoked mozzarella, which was made to be melted. The result is a velvety texture interspersed with salty chunks of ham hock.

a handful of coarse sea salt

500 g/1 lb. macaroni

190 g/6½ oz. cooked ham hock, shredded

250 g/8 oz. smoked mozzarella, finely sliced

1 quantity béchamel sauce (page 8), omitting the Monterey Jack and reducing the quantity of Cheddar to 100 g/¾ cup

50 g/1 cup fresh breadcrumbs

fine sea salt and freshly ground black pepper

SERVES 6-8

Cook the macaroni according to the instructions on page 8.

Combine the ham hock and half the mozzarella and mix well. Taste and adjust the seasoning. Set aside.

Preheat the grill/broiler to medium.

Prepare the béchamel sauce according to the instructions on page 8. Remove from the heat and add the cheese, mixing well with a spoon to incorporate. Taste and adjust the seasoning.

Put the cooked macaroni in a large mixing bowl. Pour over the hot béchamel sauce and the ham mixture and mix well. Taste and adjust the seasoning.

Transfer the macaroni mixture to a baking dish and spread evenly. Top with the remaining mozzarella and a good grinding of black pepper and sprinkle the breadcrumbs evenly over the top. Grill/broil for 5-10 minutes until the top is crunchy and golden brown. Serve immediately.

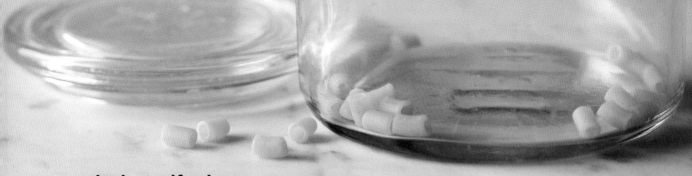

Chicken Alfredo

Somewhat retro in feel, creamy alfredo sauce flavoured with parsley lends itself well to mac 'n' cheese. Shredded, skinless roast chicken pieces give this dish a lovely, chunky texture, but cooked minced/ground chicken also works well with the shape of the macaroni, so can just as easily be used.

a handful of coarse sea salt

500 g/1 lb. macaroni

2 tablespoons vegetable oil

1 large onion, diced

500 g/1 lb. skinless and boneless poached or roasted chicken, shredded

1 quantity béchamel sauce (page 8), replacing the Monterey Jack with 100 g/1¼ cups grated Parmesan and increasing the quantity of Cheddar to 200 g/1⅔ cups

a small bunch of fresh parsley, finely chopped

50 g/1 cup fresh breadcrumbs

fine sea salt and freshly ground black pepper

SERVES 6-8

Cook the macaroni according to the instructions on page 8.

Heat the oil in a large frying pan/skillet. Add the onion and cook over high heat for about 5 minutes until brown and caramelized, stirring occasionally. Add the chicken and cook for 5–7 minutes more until just browned, stirring occasionally. Taste and adjust the seasoning. Set aside.

Preheat the grill/broiler to medium.

Prepare the béchamel sauce according to the instructions on page 8. Remove from the heat and add the cheeses and half the parsley, mixing well with a spoon to incorporate. Taste and adjust the seasoning.

Put the cooked macaroni in a large mixing bowl. Pour over the hot béchamel sauce and mix well, then stir in the chicken mixture. Taste and adjust the seasoning. Transfer the macaroni mixture to a baking dish and spread evenly. Top with a good grinding of black pepper, scatter over the remaining parsley and sprinkle the breadcrumbs evenly over the top. Grill/broil for 5–10 minutes until the top is crunchy and golden brown. Serve immediately.

BBQ Chicken & Two Cheeses

Ideal for hectic households, this straightforward combination has tastes that appeal to all generations, with the added bonus of being very quick to prepare. Serve with corn, coleslaw and a crisp green salad to go with the barbecue flavours.

a handful of coarse sea salt

500 g/1 lb. macaroni

250 g/4 oz. skinless and boneless poached or roasted chicken, shredded

250 ml/1 cup barbecue sauce

1 quantity béchamel sauce (page 8), omitting the Monterey Jack and increasing the quantity of Cheddar to 200 g/1⅔ cups

250 g/8 oz. mozzarella, half shredded and half sliced

50 g/1 cup fresh breadcrumbs

fine sea salt and freshly ground black pepper

SERVES 6-8

Cook the macaroni according to the instructions on page 8.

Put the shredded chicken and the barbecue sauce in a large bowl and mix well. Taste and adjust the seasoning. Set aside.

Preheat the grill/broiler to medium.

Prepare the béchamel sauce according to the instructions on page 8. Remove from the heat and add the Cheddar and shredded mozzarella, mixing well with a spoon to incorporate. Taste and adjust the seasoning.

Put the cooked macaroni in a large mixing bowl. Pour over the hot béchamel sauce and the chicken mixture and mix well. Taste and adjust the seasoning.

Transfer the macaroni to a baking dish and spread evenly. Top with the sliced mozzarella and a good grinding of black pepper and sprinkle the breadcrumbs evenly over the top. Grill/broil for 5-10 minutes until the top is crunchy and golden brown. Serve immediately.

Pancetta, Gorgonzola & Tomato

A strongly flavoured cheese such as Gorgonzola seems to pair better with a cream sauce rather than béchamel, though this is by no means a delicate dish, as the smoky pancetta and tomato reduction only adds to the intensity. Serve with wilted greens or roasted broccoli and a hearty Italian red wine for a sophisticated meal.

a handful of coarse sea salt

500 g/1 lb. macaroni

2 tablespoons olive oil

1 onion, finely chopped

200 g/7 oz. pancetta, chopped

½ teaspoon dried thyme

1 x 400-g/14-oz. can chopped tomatoes

a pinch of sugar

600 ml/2½ cups double/heavy cream

200 g/1½ cups crumbled Gorgonzola

50 g/1⅔ cups grated Parmesan

50 g/1 cup fresh breadcrumbs

fine sea salt and freshly ground black pepper

SERVES 6-8

Cook the macaroni according to the instructions on page 8.

Heat the oil in a large frying pan/skillet. Add the onion and cook over high heat for about 5 minutes until just caramelized, stirring occasionally. Stir in the pancetta and thyme and cook for 2-3 minutes until browned, stirring occasionally. Add the tomatoes, sugar and 1 teaspoon of fine sea salt and simmer very gently for 15-30 minutes until the mixture has reduced to a jam-like consistency. Transfer to a large bowl and set aside.

Preheat the grill/broiler to medium-hot.

Put the cream in a large saucepan and bring just to the boil, then reduce the heat. Add the cheeses and stir well to melt.

Put the cooked macaroni in the bowl with the tomato mixture. Pour over the hot cream sauce and mix well. Taste and adjust the seasoning.

Transfer the macaroni mixture to a baking dish and spread evenly. Top with a good grinding of black pepper and sprinkle the breadcrumbs evenly over the top. Grill/broil for 5-10 minutes until the top is crunchy and golden brown Serve immediately.

Serrano Ham, Smoked Paprika & Spanish Blue

This trio of flavours has long been a favourite in Spanish cooking and mac 'n' cheese is yet another excuse for putting them together. A robust and comforting dish that brings the warmth of the Mediterranean to the kitchen, this recipe is perfect for brightening up cold winter days.

Cook the macaroni according to the instructions on page 8.

Heat the oil in a large sauté pan with a lid over medium–high heat. Add the onion and red pepper and cook for about 5 minutes until the onion is just golden. Stir in the paprika, ham and garlic and cook gently for 1 minute, taking care not let the garlic burn. Add the tomatoes and wine and simmer very gently for 15–30 minutes until the mixture has reduced to a jam-like consistency. Taste and adjust the seasoning.

Preheat the grill/broiler to medium–hot.

Put the cream in a large saucepan and bring just to the boil, then reduce the heat. Add the cheeses and stir well to melt.

Put the cooked macaroni in a large bowl. Pour over the hot cream sauce, add the ham mixture and mix well. Taste and adjust the seasoning.

Transfer the macaroni mixture to a baking dish and spread evenly. Top with a good grinding of black pepper and sprinkle the breadcrumbs evenly over the top. Grill/broil for 5–10 minutes until the top is crunchy and golden brown. Serve immediately.

a handful of coarse sea salt

500 g/1 lb. macaroni

2–3 tablespoons vegetable oil

1 onion, finely chopped

1 red pepper, sliced

2 teaspoons sweet smoked paprika

100 g/3½ oz. Serrano or other cured ham, finely chopped

1 garlic clove, finely chopped

1 x 400-g/14-oz. can chopped tomatoes

60 ml/¼ cup red wine

600 ml/2½ cups double/heavy cream

200 g/1⅔ cups grated mild Cheddar cheese or Monterey Jack

100 g/¾ cup crumbled Spanish blue cheese

50 g/1 cup fresh breadcrumbs

fine sea salt and freshly ground black pepper

SERVES 6–8

index

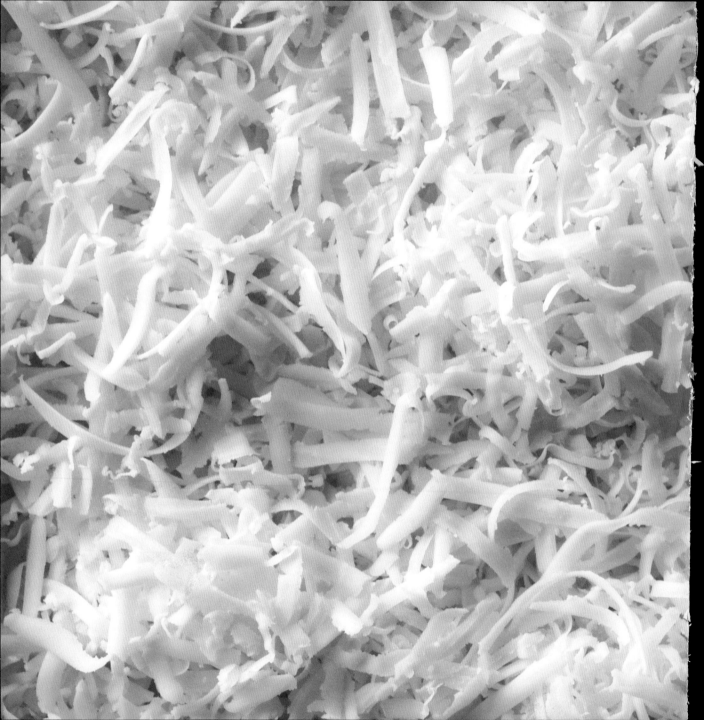